AMONG THE WILDFLOWERS

CRAIG RANDALL

switchboard
PUBLISHING

Also by Craig Randall

Fiction

The Doom that Came to Astoria: The Northwest Trilogy Part 1
The Dreams in the Pearl House: The Northwest Trilogy Part 2

Poetry

To Chase the Sun

"April, dressed in all [its] trim, has put a spirit of youth in everything."

William Shakespeare, Sonnet 98

INTRODUCTION

If you're like me, you spent most of your life wondering if the day would turn out *good* or *bad*. You assumed life was a series of arbitrary moments stirring feelings we as people had no choice but to bend to. I've never been more happy to be wrong.

Looking back, I had no idea how powerful we as people actually are. How powerful I am, and *was*. Humans are brilliant. We're capable of so much, if our surroundings allow us to believe it.

I'd spent most of my life having adopted a pessimistic outlook on life, slipping into a deep depression that lasted years. After getting medicated and shifting my perspective–a miracle in itself because I, like many, assumed that it was *just who I was*–I attempted to go off the meds...and crashed.

If you read *To Chase the Sun*, you know what happened. I slipped further into a deeper, darker despair, bleaker than I'd ever know. But I was armed with one thing I didn't have before. I'd *felt* hope and knew it could be found again.

To Chase the Sun captures the journey of finding hope

again amidst the chaos swirling through our minds to sever that connection.

Among the Wildflowers is that journey continued. Just as life changes with the seasons, this collection reflects that on a thematic level.

The breaking up of the poems was never conscious. It was simply there. As I grew and healed, the images and metaphors that took over shifted from finding hope (I'd found it again) to *keeping* it.

That became the mission. The goal. And, really, the challenge.

As mentioned above, I'd spent most of my life ushered along by the ebb and flow of what I see now were caustic and uneven winds. Emotions. Feelings that led and sat behind the driver's seat when they were never meant to be anything other than passengers. This book represents my greatest push in maintaining my own cultivation of that hope.

Don't get me wrong. That's not to say we bury them or push them down. That's been too long the norm of our culture, especially for men. No. We need to feel them. Experience them. Process them and place them where they belong, allowing us to move forward in our lives with great ease and lean into whatever life throws at us!

This, I feel, was so hidden from me for so many years. Learning to lean into it all, seeking to understand both the feelings and myself, realizing they're one, and for me, the writing unlocked it.

As much as *To Chase the Sun* focuses on imagery of Light and the Sun as representations of Hope, this collection steered me toward the next step in the process. Cultivation. As such, the majority of the images and figurative language circle around the idea of flowers and gardens and other aspects of the natural world.

The funnest part was simply watching this shift take place,

as natural as the petals of a flower opening as it starts to bloom (to stick with that metaphor again).

It's broken up into several sections referred to as patches. As in patches of flowers and growth. Each patch, a collection of images and/or thoughts that connect to each other in some natural way. For the most part these are still published in chronological order, but some were adjusted for thematic purposes.

Like *To Chase the Sun*, you will find work addressing both the dark and the light. Despair and Hope, still always with the intention of moving forward towards the sun, or in this case *blooming*.

The majority of the poems in this collection are shorter and to the point, as I had a very specific purpose in writing them. I was still bringing Order to my life. These Haiku and other short forms of verse were infinitely helpful in bringing about that peace and understanding. To risk writing longer poetry at the time would've risked losing myself again, in a way. But for those of you who loved the longer poems, never fear, there are many and will be published in future collections.

And yes, there will be future collections. The journey didn't end once hope was found. Nor did it end once I started learning to maintain it. Those are really just beginnings (a lesson in itself).

In the turbulent years of the global pandemic that followed, I went back to these poems often. Daily for certain periods of time, as testaments, ways to remember the growth and progress I'd made. To remember the trajectory I'd been on. To find that path again.

To find the line I'd cultivated so deeply in my mind, where the sun could still shine and all the flowers could still bloom.

Writing what became this collection reinforced the realization, daily, that I can plant what thoughts I want into my mind and hew the peace I want to feel. I could, and *can*, root myself where I needed to be, and I could thrive.

The most pressing thing to me, when I write this now, is knowing we forget. It's not a *good* or a *bad* thing, it's just a *thing* about people.

Among the Wildflowers, to me, is a reminder. A reminder of what's possible. Of what we're each capable of accomplishing. It's a reminder of the lives we live when fully alive. A reminder I will come back to for years to come and rest upon.

I hope this book can be even a sliver of that for you. That within it you will find encouragement and empathy. I hope that you will find yourself in these pages, beauty and blemishes and all! I hope that it can be a reminder to you that healing, hope, and light exist, for each of us and that all can be made whole again if we have the courage to let go.

Remember to take care where you plant yourself, and always remember how powerful you are.

Patch One: Untamed Soil

A Life of Hope

I want to live a
life of hope, well beyond the
confines of my fear

Blankets

let forgiveness fall
like snow; its gentle touch will
blanket every wound

Defined Shores

my mind is an ocean;
left without defined shores it
will envelop all

Jealous Rain

have you considered
the jealousy of rain; it
yearns for warm embrace

The Mind pt. 2

tidal
currents swiftly
spread through
varying city
streets

citizens
flee, forced
to new homes

Reflection

I was not broken,
just a reflection of a
world so deep in need

I See You, My Friend

I see you, my friend,
holding onto grief as a
cloud holds to its tears

Bright Scars: a tanka

my scars are like the
stars above, bright and numbered,
though hidden behind
the well intentioned cover
of obscuring midnight skies

Whether It Be True

I've often wondered
whether it be true that I
was born to overcome

Willingness to Shine

what if the sun put
conditions upon its
willingness to shine

Returned Intact

I have traveled to
the furthest depths of self and
have returned intact

Invisible Selves: a tanka

at times we are the
ghosts of others' lives, left not
to be remembered -
but only if unseen by
self are we invisible

Edge of Mourning

I stand on the edge
of mourning while the dawn shakes,
beck'ning me awake

Let It Be Worth More

do not burden hope
by living for lesser dreams;
let it be worth more

Resist

the confines of these
prison walls are kept strong
by leaning into lies

Autumn Turns

autumn turns,
with courage, to face the
inevitable

Even the Sky Needs Rest

even the sky needs
release and rest; we weren't meant
to carry ev'rything

Darkness Cannot Cast

I am thankful that
the darkness cannot cast its
shadow on the light

Hope is What Remains

hope is what remains
when we grow wise—or weary—
enough to let go

Patch Two: Cultivating

Among the Wildflowers

I will lay my head
and rest my soul among the
wildflower fields

In the Stillness

in the stillness I
do sense the stirring of my
spirit growing bold

Quaking Thoughts

I will sit and learn
to still my mind and bring calm
to these quaking thoughts

Intention: a tanka

I will build my hopes
upon the certainty of
all I know as true,
upon the certainty of
the coming of the new dawn

To Tame the Mind

to tame the mind is
deepest purpose and quickest
path to peace and heart

My Heart Aches, In Me

my heart aches, in me,
for expansive spaces to
roam and run—to *be*

Hope is What Burns

hope is what burns so
deep within, setting fire to
spirit, mind, and soul

Thank You, My Love, My Heart

thank you my heart, my
hope, and my love, for leaving
the light on for me

Song of Morning

I long to hear the
song of morning, it's rhythm,
illumination

Set Your Heart to Hope

set your gaze, your mind,
 your heart to hope, then watch
morning rise and reign

Let's Not Grieve the Rain

let's not grieve the rain,
it falls by grace and prepares,
for us fertile soil

Steadfast is the Strength of Hope

steadfast is the strength
of hope, and sturdy when we
find ourselves in need

PATCH THREE: ROOTED

Among the Wildflowers pt 2

I will root myself
among the wildflowers,
among such seeds of hope

My Heart and Home

no matter where we
plant our feet, you will always
be my heart and home

The Most Resilient Seed

hope is the most
resilient seed; it can be
planted in any soil

Hold Strong to Deep Roots

lean in, like a tree
into the wind, hold strong to
the deep roots—endure

Only You Can Let Them

only you can let
them steal your peace, so plant it
deep in starlit fields

Stand 'til True

Most the blooms I see in fields
Hold to their roots in painful strain
Unaware the powers they wield
Unaware they'll come again

Hold to their roots in painful strain
The blooms do fear their beauty's fade
Unknowing they will come again
Unknowing they will be remade

The blooms do fear their beauty's fade
Yet Wildflowers stand 'til true
Knowing they will be remade
To spread their wonder, beauteous hue

The Wildflowers stand 'til true
Below deep skies of calming blues,
To spread their wonder, beauteous hues,
Off'ring hope to hold and trust for you

I Have Deepest Need

I have deepest need
of roots, so as to weather
every drought and storm

The Most Rooted Blooms

the most rooted blooms
of spring will last and learn to
see another sun

Your Tears Will Water Seeds

fear not, for your tears
will water seeds to root and
raise much needed life

PATCH FOUR:
MINUTIAE

Leonard

I've missed you more than you could know
And wonder if my hopes you hear,
Those words that spill out of the soul,
Those thoughts of heart so close, so near.

I often pray that proud you'd be
When look you will, below, at me,
And hurt not that I forward must—
In lov'd memories I trust.

Daisy

the fox, it hides down
in its hole, pressing backward
against these coming forces

yet, in the open
fields above, the daisy's arms
reach up high and wide

Sacred: a gogyohka

there is something
sacred about your
child falling asleep in the
safety and comfort of
your arms

Left in Want

an empty park bench
waits long for weary patrons,
pigeons left un-fed

At Play

watch the freedom of
a child at play; such is
the way we need live

.

Spring Rain

spring rain,
even so, the sun streaks still
break through

A Sparrow Calls

on the wire
a sparrow calls out to the day,
weightless

Let Each Story Carry

lost from page to page
I let each story carry
me unto resolve

Then Will Rise the Sleepy Sun

when the stars fade and
slumber calls them down, then will
rise the sleepy sun

Some Days are for Rest

some days are for rest,
lounging 'round the house, relaxed,
lackadaisical

Sing, For Years to Come

this will mark the day—
it will sing for years to come—
and speak of what *was*

Morning Ascent

the sun makes its
ascent as the birds call out
to one another

Cherry Blossoms

the cherry blossoms
are returning to mark the
birth of this new year

Portland Summers

Portland summers,
waterfront blues and sunset
walks down Belmont street

PATCH FIVE:
WEATHERING

Sunless Sky

I would rather live
beneath a sunless sky than
close my heart to hope

Does Not the Flower Suffer

does not the flower
suffer while it wilts, yet will
regain what was lost

The Clever Sun

the clever sun has
found its way into the night,
filling dark with light

The Voice of Spring

springtime speaks to me
of what has been—of loss, of
gain—hope amidst the hurt

It Matters Not

it matters not if
the rains fall hard when I can
conjure suns to mind

The Tides Will Ebb and Flow

the tides will ebb and
flow as they choose, but peace is
always found within

Rest Your Weary Bones

rest your weary bones;
aren't you tired and worn from
holding up the rain?

Together, We

together, we will
make it through and endure the
subtle season's change

The Winter Sun

the resilience of
the winter sun gives courage
to my withered heart

Be Bold

let the sun set on
all that undermines your soul;
life is much too short

Could a Sunrise Steal

have you ever seen a
sunrise that could not help but
steal away the pain?

Some Days Are

some days are filled with
sadness—with no sun—but can
still be filled with hope

Leafless Trees

I choose to see the
leafless trees as promises
of what's next to come

We Sing, Yet

we sing of spring time's
longing warmth, yet winter's frost,
too, has need of song

Until Tomorrow

we were born to
weather storms, to endure
until tomorrow

Hold Fast

hold fast and steady
against the wiles of the
world, do not be moved

Take Captive Hold

take captive hold to
ev'ry thought, lest they become,
each, your prison walls

PATCH SIX: IN BLOOM

Among the Wildflowers pt 3

Among the wildflowers and their sweet breeze
My heart is full and pressed to burst,
A soul so rooted, deep to please;
Among the wildflowers and their sweet breeze
I lay my head and rest at ease;
I am alive in well met thirst;
Among the wildflowers and their sweet breeze,
My heart is full and pressed to burst

In Bloom

isn't a garden
most beautiful when ev'ry
flower is in bloom?

Akin in Beauty

the wildflowers
belong to you, akin are
you both in beauty

The Wind it Weaves its Way Through Fields of Gold

The wind it weaves its way through fields of gold,
The slowness of its turns do beg me sit,
Its warmth was made to bless the young and old.

Horizon lines frame scenery and fold,
As corresponding sky and tree lines fit,
The wind it weaves its way through fields of gold.

My spirit comes alive by nature's hold,
Its signature across my soul is writ,
Its warmth was made to bless the young and old.

My body and my mind obeys as told;
They thread their way through waves the years have knit,
The wind it weaves its way through fields of gold.

In places far from time's constraining mold,
Forever, here I'd stay if I had wit,
Its warmth was made to bless the young and old.

With patient ears of heart, I mustn't quit,
ever searching something more—I must admit:
The wind it weaves its way through fields of gold,
Its warmth was made to bless the young and old.

Let Rivers Run the Banks Ashore

When boundaries push to hold us in,
Prevent our souls their need to soar,
A need there is for hope to win—
Let rivers run the banks ashore.

Encroach they will, recede in time,
If left alone they will restore,
'tis up to us to hold the line—
Let rivers run the banks ashore.

For shallow do our depths become,
When widening will lift the floor,
If fight we don't for room to run—
Let rivers run the banks ashore.

So carve out of the day our needs,
Whatever lets us loose and roar,
Whatever lets our souls be freed—
Let rivers run the banks ashore.

Once Untrodden Fields

These paths we walk were once untrodden fields;
so lush, they bare the fruit of thoughtful choice,
carved out of time as step's intention wields—
the tracks of which we leave to prove our voice.

Alas, the Song of Morning Comes

alas, the song of
morning comes, and with it the
sweetest scent of dew

The Skies are Clear Today

the skies are clear
today, leaving no impediments
for the rushing wind

The Heart of Spring

deep down, I know the
heart of spring, that, like me, it
yearns to be reborn

Wildflower Moon

I shout loud to lift
my soul as I walk beneath the
wildflower moon

Patch Seven: Alive and Full

Sail Beyond

I will sail atop
the wild winds to travel
well beyond my dreams

Stardust

feed my soul with
stardust pure and tempt
me not with less

Whisper Unto Me: a tanka

whisper unto me
the truth and depths of who I
am; breathe life back in-
to embers cool—and warmth; then
come to watch the fires rise

So Close to Far

I am not lost—nor
am I found so close to far
But at peace and free

The Coming of the Dawn

can you see it,
the coming of the dawn,
bold horizon's fire

Live and Love

from children may we
learn to love—to live within
the precious moments

Twelve Years On

Though sunburns over years have tendency to fade,
A heart full-pierced will have its need for longing love;
If stay we underneath of August's shine above,
A love complete, uncompromising have we made.

Now, twelve years on I must confess I love you more,
Than any other time I've known, while looking back;
Through hardships, times of joy, or when the mind's lost track,
August's orbit pulls us tightly to where before.

You, my love, are where I've been, always, most at home;
The beauty of your soul, your heart, it shines beyond,
Something deeper than the burn we share, our ties, our bond,
Begun that fateful day when August's burn first showed.

Joyful is our life entwined—my love—my heart is won,
In spending all these years with you beneath the sun.

Astoria to Amsterdam

Astoria to
Amsterdam my heart, my love,
always knit to yours

My Children, Remember

To you, my children, brave and bold
Always remember to live free
Let go the strings and lies of old
Never forget to simply be

Always remember to live free
Of shackled rules that others make
Never forget to simply be
Save you it will from growing ache

Of shackled rules that others make
Always remember who you are
Save you it will from growing ache
Bring back to home if drifted far

Let go the strings and lies of old
Of shackled rules that others make
To you, my children, brave and bold
Save you it will from growing ache

Beneath a Starry Sky

have you ever stood
beneath a starry sky and
dreamt of worlds beyond?

Spark of Life

do you feel the spark,
how the thunder strikes your
very bones to life?

Flame and Fire

the night sky kindles
fire and flame, igniting
something deep within

Behold, the Wonder of it All

at times, I step back
and behold the wonder of
it all—breath runs short

I Belong With You, My Love

I belong with you,
my love, upon the gentle
seas, sun kissed, and free

Home Is a Hearth Well Warmed

home is a hearth well
warmed by the presence of those
we hold close and love

The *Now* is Ripe

the *now* is ripe with
feeling, the buzz of what each
next moment might bring

To Be Human: a tanka

to be human is
to be a creat've force, to
be a hurricane,
to be alive and out of
reach of all that quells the mind

Room For New

I take heart that each
season sees fit to step aside,
making room for new

To Be Whole

to be whole
is not to *be* complete,
but at peace

Abolitionist

I aim to be the
abolitionist of my
spirit, mind, and soul

Let Life Breathe

let life breathe, let
it course and flow where it will;
then it will *take*—soar

Today, Be the Reason

today, be the
reason someone smiles, that
they believe, hope

My Soul is Strong

my soul is strong;
it was built to last beyond,
infinite

Upon the Table Spinning

I am not broken
but a bowl-of-clay upon
the table spinning

The Twilit Stars

the twilit stars do
usher in the night, and guide our
dreams on to their homes

AFTERWORD

Thank you for reading. It means the world to me that you would take the time to meander through these little bouquets of words I chiselled together to better understand myself and the world.

I hope they sang to you as writing them did for me, and that they opened your eyes and your heart to life's possibilities.

This book represents part two in a healing journey I've been on. The next of which went in directions I could never have predicted.

Like it did for most people, COVID 19 pretty much decimated any plans I'd made. I felt the themes in my work start to change again, as they did between To Chase the Sun and Among the Wildflowers, but as that change happened, the pandemic spread around the globe, spiralling my healing journey, and this reflective work in wild directions.

The result came in the form of my next collection, Rain Songs, which will be published in the Fall of 2023. I cannot wait to share it. Where as this book and its predecessor lean into the light with all their strength, Rain Song seeks to hold life with more balanced hands. It taught me so much and allowed me to process my way through a pandemic, riots, unrest, brutality, as well as continue my journey of hope and healing. Until then.

Thank you.

Craig Randall, October 2022

JOIN THE NEWSLETTER